*the paths one takes
in searching for oneself
for one's past
become, like a map,
the key to this past
the roots of one's life
the routes of one's search*

for Sheila Watson
and Corinne McLuhan
. . . routes through
unmapped territory

ROUTES/ROOTS

By
Elizabeth McLuhan

Griffin House
Toronto 1974

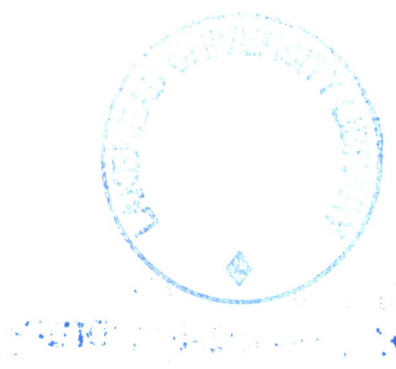

© Elizabeth McLuhan / 1974

Published by Griffin Press Limited
461 King Street West, Toronto, Canada
M5V 1K7

All rights reserved. No part of this book may be reproduced, transmitted in any form or by any means, electronic, mechanical photocopying, recording, or otherwise, or stored in a retrieval system without the written permission in advance of the publisher.

ISBN 0 88760 068 9

Cover photos by Barbara Wilde

The author gratefully acknowledges permission to reprint some of the poems in this collection which appeared previously in *White Pelican*

Printed in Canada

When day and life draw the horizons
Part of the strangeness is
Knowing the landscape.

Margaret Avison, "From A Provincial"
The Dumbfounding

The wish to be mid forest grass
Autumn: by wild-fires burned
Annihilation: is there no pain?
The wish for root connection

Ts'ao Chih, "Alas"
*... the silent Zero,
   in search of Sound ...*

calm

in the eye

of the storm

and cold

I watching

myself drown

eyedull thoughts

eye can see you
but eye cannot get near you

it is clear that eye
can only try to tell you

                if you are dumb
                eye cannot hear you

                if you are deaf
                eye can but spell you

                if you are warm
                eye cannot share you

                if you come close
                eye cannot smell you

                if you are blind
                eye can but fear you

July, 1969

what I noticed
if not first
then noticed
most
was that
your fingers
were thick but long
the skin soft
and so crumpled
that the finger joints
were so many closed mouths
staring thick lipped
and solemn   your hands
remained motionless

there is nothing
to be said you said

then the silent hands
by which no movement
was sudden no movement
was explained
lifted me up lay me down
and a dozen mouths
descended singing silent

November, 1972

you bend
towards me
your breath
the odour of over
ripe oranges
your kiss dry
thin-lipped
old discarded
peelings

you are not old

when was all
the life
squeezed out
of you?

how long have your drained
features been
moving closer
moving with a thirst
to drink me dry?

the smell
of oranges
grows heavy
then
subsides

December, 1972

does anyone have the time of day?

I carry it with me
in my pocket
tucked carefully under
candy wrappers and
crumpled kleenex

I kill time in my own small way

I have time
in my head
so carefully
carved up
that no one ever sees

the scars on everything I say

time is coiled
round my wrists
in strings that
strangle seconds
and make it hard
to play

that force me to my knees to pray

the sands of time
fall heavy
in my head
they sift
through all my senses
and slowly bury
what I used to be

I feel myself sink deeper every day

February, 1969

there was a song
I used to sing
when I was young
and all alone
I'd whisper it
to empty rooms
or shout it
at the quiet phone

there was a game
I learned to play
when I was scared
and very small
I'd draw smiles
on people's faces
and then pin them
to the wall

                    there were some words
                    I found to say
                    when I grew up
                    and couldn't play
                    I'd tell each man
                    I met from
                    time to time
                    that what
                    was mine
                    was his
                    and his
                    was mine

January, 1969

you took my hand
and called me Child
and summoned me
to stay a while
you said I should not
live alone and
dance at night
beneath the moon
you told me
life was full of pain
and once hurt,
I'd be hurt
again

because you cared
you'd show me
how to see
the misery of life
and what I'd be

then, Child,
you whispered,
God's not here
he's just a
substitute
for fear
and don't you know
that those called
Friends are only
those who best pretend?
for all I tell you
now is true
what befell me
will come to you

and then you led me
to your room
you seemed so happy
in the gloom
you kissed me
as you'd drive a nail
you held me till
your hatred failed

so I stayed with you
till my love was spent
but now the night is late

and, Child,
it's time I went

March, 1969

in the deepening darkness of a dying night
as your dreams descend the staircase of your sleep
then you know whatever happens now or might
you can't collect the hopes you didn't keep

still you wonder what your dreams are all about
and why you dread the coming of the dawn
your eyes are looking in and looking out
your black cat in the corner blinks then yawns

and how'd you ever get so torn and messed
you'd always thought that all your seams were straight
and you're waiting at the station with the rest
but tomorrow's train already is too late

November, 1969

I never told you where I came from
you never thought to ask
we'd been nowhere but the place to which we'd come
we photographed each moment as it passed

I never told you what I'd ever done
you said you only cared what I did now
but without my past my present was struck dumb
silent sentences were all I had to show

I never told you who I was
you said you saw the answer in my face
and though our thoughts were never bound by laws
our smiles hung in the air like heavy weights

I never told you where I wished to go
you only asked how long I would remain
yourself was all you really cared to know
I was just another place that you could name

March, 1969

to sit
and talk
of things
and of events
delays the moment
that must finally come
the awkward emptiness
the silent present tense

full ripe
with revelation
of reality and sense

how fingers hum
and skins communicate
their scents
and thoughts
float free
in pools
within the eyes

and words
so wasted once
and dense

lie quiet now
and as they die
repent

June, 1970

golden

he was a golden boy
shiny faced and golden locked
hair bright as polished mirrors
golden knots
          rushing like a
hundred curling waves upon
his head and down his neck
a hundred curling waves
poised reticent to break

upon the strand
upon his back's
soft golden sand

he
with the
golden throat
would sing when
he couldn't talk
walk when he
couldn't stand
on his golden notes

December, 1972

self reflection
flattens out your face
reduces all your
curves to lines
that cannot
be erased

your mirror
is a magic box
transforming
all your fright
your image has
a hundred locks

you suffocate
at night

May, 1971

it wasn't that you meant to crack the shell
it wasn't that you tried to break the spell
it's not her heart that you're not worthy of
it was only that you tried to show your love

and all the while her smile was never bent
but inch by inch her body shrank then went
yet it wasn't that she didn't really care
but her body never had before been bared

and her body was the bar across her mind
she feared you'd strip her thoughts
leave her behind

July, 1969

go now the night is done
my love evaporates beneath
the mourning sun
my love is deep blue ice
and thrives in darkness
it pulls in others
with a touch so cold
they think I burn
like fire

January, 1971

master-baiting

you'd never know
I'm a creature of creations
you'll never know
how long it took to make you
all the hours
that were spent in machinations
all the parts it took
on my part to chrome plate you

you'd never know
I'm a slave who trains her masters
you'll never know
how I struggled to create you
all the hours
spent in detailed drawn disasters
now that you're finally ready
I can hate you

July, 1970

child you mustn't look so hard
you mustn't look so hard
for things that don't exist
you search for semblances of sanity
on the faces of the inmates in the ward
but sanity's their sickness
and they spread it with a kiss

child you mustn't cry at night
you mustn't cry at night
from the noises that you hear
it's only rattling the cages
you revere
it's only dark
that tells you
what you fear
is light

child you mustn't try to speak
you mustn't try to speak
and even if you could
what would you say
you know that strength is silence
but your words are weak
and weariness the warden
makes you stay

singing wild
you beat your fists upon the door
singing singing singing wild
singing child
you stamp your feet upon the floor
singing singing singing child

you scream your song
trying to tear it free
and rid yourself
of monsters that you see

singing wild
you're trying to remember
singing singing singing wild
singing child
this time you won't surrender
singing singing singing child

the words roll out
the music flees your mind
the notes are all like bullets
bursting through your wall of time

singing wild
you're balanced on a line
singing singing singing wild
singing child
don't look down another time
singing singing singing child

now the words are winged and crazy
birds that flap around the room
the music brings no answers
only intervals of tune

singing wild
you'll sing yourself to death
singing singing singing wild
singing child
you lived too long
inside your head
singing singing singing child

August, 1969

is it this then?
a fly tacked to the wall?

multicoloured black
embalmed and winged
grey gauze and thread
with many sided eyes
the sighted spheres
that tack your captors
to a stare
but no eyelids to deny
that what you see
is always there

exercising imitations
of the way their captives crawl
your creeping captains curse
and tack each other to the wall
as you watch secure and suffer

with no tack you'd surely fall

April, 1971

I'll name you
that will make you smaller
put you in writing
till you holler
from the blankness
of your paper sell

                    (a name engulfs you
                       and it starts to gell

                       a sort of semantic cement
                       used by those who are
                       powerbent
                       tools of those who are
                       heaven sent   )

I'll name you tame you
to bend beneath my wit
labelled, fabled
you'll grow to like the fit

December, 1970

o lady of the symbols
o father with no face
o mother of the master
o master of the race

I am twisting I am turning
but the road remains so straight
I am walking I am running
o my father am I late?

the moon has turned to crystal
and the sun is growing black
the sky is full of starfish
o my lady take me back

I've only asked you questions
father — never wanted favours
I've offered you black roses
I've made love to your saviours

but now my saints are scattered
and my grace is growing thin
o my father o my lady
is it possible I've sinned?

I am walking through the fire
I am tossing on the waves
I am calling to you father
but I still can't see your face

my confession is my clothing
my penance is my god
my father are you smiling?
o my lady do you nod?

February, 1970

and when the time comes
or when it's time to go
then time seems real
but there is no
present moment
no point at which one says
it's three o'clock I feel

no way in which to know
what time it is
no way to stop the clock
or stop oneself
living is time's beanstalk
and one has to grow
as though to reap a harvest
that just living sowed
a huge now limp
old leafy thing
a product of one's time
that didn't show
itself at first

one grew but couldn't feel
times come and go
couldn't see the stalk
grow taller
or the leaves
unfold

October, 1970

          it came one day
exploded in my head
a silent Hiroshima
mushroom form dissolving
and dispersing throughout
my entire atmosphere
my body's nations
and my nervous networks
splintered and disrupted
connections all cut dead

does it matter who finally pushed the button?

my aching leg
the dizzy spell
the crazy cracking headache
no matter now
I am done
the little atom bomb
inside me
had no alternate escape
I'd stored it and ignored it
far too long

it's had its day in infamy
now my blood glistens
with its poison
bones ring
with its fatal song

and how I pull myself together
picking up the rubble and debris
carefully arranging it
like some old whore
primping before a mirror
—me—the mistress of my madness
and how the marquis grins
how my little histories
(beloved bastards)
grow hysterical
are screaming from the pain
radiation burned and scarred almost beyond recognition
they limp and crawl within my brain

such a catastrophe
and no one knows it's happened
except me—and
—to all appearances
I was only home alone
again watching tv

October, 1970

your wet words hang
like drops of water
from an eavestrough
after a storm
and then they
fall in orders
from your rusted mouth
and you think she's listening
to the crimes you cough
as you lash yourself
with whips of wishful lies
and blood runs from the love
you will not recognize
but things have changed
you see your love
no longer cries

and you call to her
across the space
of interrupted time
and you cry
you can't leave now
you know your love is mine

but already she is gone
your eyes are suddenly
struck blind
and now you sit alone
cross-legged across the room
your mind is dead
your body is a tomb
your dirge drones on
in words without a tune
your epitaph will read
you died too soon
but no one comes to visit
save the moon

March, 1969

Copyrighted for music, 1970

sing sweet
and sad
and soft
lie high
and low
and rest
your aching feet
sing of the tears
you saved
in purple jars
the nights
are long
the days go by
like years

sing sweet
and sad
and soft
and rest
your weary head
and close your eyes
sing of the birds
that fly
and men
who creep
the seconds
are much slower
now it seems

sing sweet
and sad
and soft
of this
and that
of a seashore
that you saw
when just
a lad
before
your time
stopped ticking
on the wall
before you found
you wanted so much more
before you came here
dying after all

March, 1970

remember me
as I remember you
with fragments of your glances
scraps of skin

and time caught—frozen
—in between the sheets

words put on ice
for temporary peace

such cold mechanics calculate
the cost to make you grin
can make you come and go
again...again...again

my memory can run the real half-speed
remembering to record
the times we meet
               dismember gestures
               moments

            I'll steal you
                     piece by piece

September, 1971

you leave
are always leaving
me to stand
a pillar
of cold ash
frozen
to the street
and looking
back
again

May, 1971

a vagueness

an uneasy unknown

factor floats about

infests the air

we breathe

hangs in our mouths

whether we whisper

or we shout

or maybe it's

within us

oozing out

I know
when I start running
down a gloomy hall
or up a sand-spilt shore
that I am going nowhere
but to an iron door
that bars the end
of every daily maze
that opens to a room
of hollow cheers where
fanfare paper effigies
are raised
on ten-foot wooden posts
ten times a year
and left until
our worship is complete
until it's time to pull them down
and heap them on the flames
where they will burn to ashes
that we eat and smear upon our faces
while asking for their names
then flail our arms about in empty air —
warding off a beast
that isn't there

and claw the bloodless brick-built walls
until our empty hands are worn to bones
until our memory's dead beyond recall
and we lift our voices
high in monotones

and cry
o where
o where
have all
our heroes
gone?

January, 1969

I dream
a dream
at night
when I forget
I dream
a dream
of songs
and ships at sea
I dream
a dream
of pinks
and lily-whites
I dream
a dream
of children
fair and free

but then
I wake
to sounds
of marching feet
I wake
again
to memorize
a fear
I wake
to see
our sanity retreat
I wake
to the explosion
of a tear

March, 1969

Adapted to music and play by W. Watson, 1969
Used on a documentary-public affairs show, 1969

chop gently as you kill
for think of all the blood that you might spill
upon your spotless hands
chop gently

kill extra if you must but not too few
your customers are pleased with what you do
and they all want their policies renewed
kill extra

starve quiet when not fed
for the faintest cry of pain might wake the dead
or stir the living
starve quiet

no matter what you see be silent
it's not life but only news that's really violent
or so the hangman said
be silent

February, 1969

mother earth

watch
as that greasy fat lady
who used to work for the circus
starts to laugh
and laugh
at something she must know
and laugh and laugh
and still the laughter grows
until her body shakes
from side to awful side
her hundred bellies roll
and her mouth is open wide

till suddenly
the mass of flesh begins to glow
with burning heat and
the fat starts sinking
to the flabby feet
until the trick is practically complete
as everyone looks on
at the lady being melted
by the sun

as she disappears into the ground
she screams   you'll pay
for what you've done

February, 1969

now I understand
there's Michael man-angel
with magic music in his hands
and every note's a coat of many colours
self sent to sing to bring his skyful songs
to all his brothers
and when he sings sweet incense scents the air
and his words fall feather fine on empty ears
and when he stops his brothers' empty eyes
are torn with tears

now I understand
there's Michael man-angel
with nails run through his hands
who calls to heaven from his concrete cross
self sent he tried to give the love
his living would release
and false accused by us who hold the price
of peace is hardly worth the cost
that greed is gain and loving is a loss
we stuck our thorny thoughts into his head
we stripped him whipped him till his beauty bled
sent him staggering through the lies that we would spread
and when he fell we kicked him so he'd crawl
till all our wars were won and love was lost
till finally we nailed him to his cross

but now a blinding black
the thunder cracks our minds grow dark with fright
and dreaded dreams awake and walk the night
and heaven's heart hears Michael crying out for light
and heaven's hand plucks Michael from our sight

August, 1969

and they packed
themselves
into concrete and steel
structures
rectangles
squares
all gagging
geometrically
they lived
there
thinking
they were really
breathing
thinking
that all their
calculations
were correct

that those who did not calculate
were not civilized
yet . . .
that the calculation
must be inculcated

and they crucified
cultures

and still they squatted
in concrete
cities
in steel
sepulchres
consecrated to their
calculations

and so
crusades
were waged
and wars
were won

and Order
was their law
and their law
was their love

and they loved everyone

June, 1969

Ode to a PR Man

a prospering prophet
with proper propensity
to print propaganda
on pious propinquity
of profit and pain

pries open the pathway
that proffers protection
for pilgrims' parades
and the primate's
projection

March, 1969

wants upon a time
too lovers were sating
on the sofar, whim
soddenly one stood
open said
        I wan two be allone

July, 1969

the Word
will waste away
in dusty ruins of an old man's mind
while choirs and congregations
sing it to death in unison
to the humdrum beat of some magician's hymn
and behind us two deaf organists
pound mary melodies of a single God
in many masquerades
whose notes rise up in rings
above our heads
and then we know
we're saints

and still
we sing
with all our prayerbook piety
until parade time comes
and up the aisles we go
we go   we go   we go
in double crippled lines
to eat the Word
to know the Lord
so we can later spew Him out
in bits and pieces as we please
against the stained glass walls
until our chanting voices
reach a fever pitch
that bends the very doors

until the wooden man
nailed to a wooden cross
can stand no more
and with resounding crack
splits into two
and falls
in splinters to the floor
and a satin priest steps up
and speaks of snakes and stars
and all the while he plays
his Bible like a drum
so high above us in his ivory pulpit
he tells us to forgive each foe
then names them in a list
in case we might not know
exactly who they are

January, 1969

I

the crazy faced madonna
staring cow
the wearing whiles
the nearing now
the thank you and god damn you
and be careful how
the primadonna belladonna ball
immortal miss
the fractured face
and cracked lip kiss
a myth as good as a smile
and still she holds the bloated child

stale bred flat wine
and whining pointed prayer
the public prays
aimed at the beast
the pubic prey
the phallic would
but cannot see the forest
or the trees
the uninvited guest
on time
a fallow feast

the holy host
on high
the parasite
sight-ridden
site-foreseen
paravoid partners
I and Thou
night visitors
who stir the sleeping cow

the I for I
the cue for cue
to form a line
aligne each form
the Bible book review
B-rated bull
to be or not to be
from Holy See
to pew
predict the past
await the present
a gift of God
the Son shone brightly
didn't last
salvation served
a pheasant under glass
a brief repast

the marvels in man's head
the all time fables
the things he could have done
but wasn't able
the masquerades and mazes
planet plays and plans to pay
are dealt with now and done
the Son has set
his cards upon the table

II

it won't be long
it won't be long
in the land of laws
and orders
the land with hidden
clause and borders

the war did more
to bring life
back to news
relieve the sordid-bored
compile and then confuse
revile and then diffuse
the daily views

the headlines:
write the wrongs
and send them all to bed

blood D-day
bomb embalmed
pay the piper
site the psalm
it wasn't long
it wasn't long
in the land of cause
recorders
the land of tragic
flaw enforcers
so come to pray
o come to pray
those who razed the living
to the ground
have come to praise the dead
without a sound

moth balls

blind you said
the men are blind to all
they fail to see the large
and miss the small

since you once spoke
time has passed it seems
and men are known
to drown within their dreams

blind you said
they're blind in every way

the men are dead
what you mistook for blindness
was decay
still you stand
instructing every corpse
and croon to them
of cosmic mother's laws
your insect eye
vivisects the sky

and carefully
you plot the paths
of moths

May, 1970

owed to a dirty old man

you arrive
like a mechanic
tool kit of ideas in hand

you are a specialist
and come right to the point

you are a plumber
who knows precisely
where the trouble is
and the trouble is always
tailor made to fit your tools

you think of yourself
as a service of sorts
you know the ins and outs

like an old scissors-sharpener
monotonously swinging your bell
you know what you come for

the old scissors-sharpener
nobody needs but
everybody gives work

still you think the world
would grow dull without you

November, 1972

see the pretty people on the streets
separate walls all walking
separate beats

families snug inside their different homes
father mother child
in different rooms

faces speaking in the normal way
with changing masks
for changing times of day

and when death is delivered by the Fates
the wooden men are sunk
in wooden crates

November, 1968

the sport of kings
is making kingdoms
made of little men
ruled by the tall

passtime of the masses
being little men
who watch the big ones fall

May, 1970

the vold skrinkled
men set thinselves
down on the partbents
mumberling to thenselves
about daze of told

July, 1969

sinking

back to

sightlessness

to smell

to sound

and armless

in the arid air

feet sunk

beneath

the ground

in the desert
the body is a bone
all sentiment is starved
thought's skin
grows dry and hard
in the desert
the body is the home
weathered down
to its unchanging part
rocking in the rhythms
of the sands
the textures of the dark
in the desert
and neither more nor less—
a part stripped clean
bleached white
beneath the scouring light
of desert's day
the cold sharp
razor's edge
of desert's night

Albuquerque, New Mexico, October, 1971

the mountains quiet giants
sprawled and lying in the sand

the city: crumpled cryptogram
junkyards of symbols
rise from giant hands

.

Albuquerque, New Mexico, September, 1971

in such desert dryness
words moist with meaning
are suddenly tossed about
like loose sands in the wind
sound has no significance
but to echo the air's hum
monotonous under
a monotonous sun
words suddenly
become dry crystals
semantic mosaics
that the wind
rearranges
growing arid
often discarded
in little heaps
like anthills
crackling beneath
the heel of the heat

Albuquerque, New Mexico, October, 1971

what is there
to make with sand
and a hard dry wind?
what certainties can be constructed
out of crumbling rocks?

instead
the landscape overwhelms
I lack the desert skills
shall I move quickly?
dart about like a roadrunner?
or stand immobile
short bristled tentacles
reading the air like braille?
assuming only one posture
a cactus but noble in rigidity?

the sun terrifies
sucks the senses dry
the ground crackles
and ants programmed in panic
manufacture microcosms
the rich blue sky
beckons like a cool sea
near but intangible
in such heat my eyes
reach like hungry children
for the liquid blue

all is mirage
colours camouflage texture
the sky is not a sea but
a dry vacuum that pulls you forward
the sand is not a soft velvet bed
but sharp crystals biting at the skin
when can I begin
to make the desert mine?

farther out mesas
and low hills erupt
dark mountains choke
beneath the sun
colours are transformed
at its will
light and dark
impose a geometric grid
over all
bleached white skulls crown
the fence posts
beyond private metamorphosis
part of a pattern now
I look but am not free
rooted more every day
to the earth
from which nothing grows
I too cast shadows
as part of the show

chalk dry with heat
all thought disintegrates
the memory dies of thirst
my heavy shoulders slouch
I harden
grown boulder
broader now
stretching out
across the sand
belonging to the desert
with the desert in my hands

Albuquerque, New Mexico, October, 1971

reach out and touch
the night's black body
her stars glisten
like beads of sweat
upon her silky skin

too soon
she spots you
swallows you
within her alabaster eye

Toronto, February, 1969

the night she covers me
she holds me close
the night she is anonymous
yet near
the night she belches blackness
she's a ghost

being no one
she is
every
one
I fear

Toronto, May, 1970

coming
softly
as a sigh
at dawn
when night
is gone
and morning
not begun
a hand
rests gentle
fallen petal
on the ground
a voice
a breeze
that scatters
fallen leaves

London, June, 1970

November lacks music
gray and still as a stone
October's only child
almost still born
to grow a darkly daughter
barren sown

October's burning trees
whose leaves of colours sang
the drunken trees
that flung their harvests down
stand skeletal now
a forest of charred bones

Toronto, November, 1972

when the first snow descends
perforates the air
without a sound
the landscape warms
arches its back and purrs
before the snow has barely
touched the ground

blanketing sharp angles
with a sudden sigh
of airspun down
snow makes interiors
of all outdoors
groundline merges with
the puffy whiteness of the sky
becoming padded walls
and ceiling
to a padded floor

I stare   I know
I think of nothing
but the white
the lie-me-down soft
stillness of the snow

Toronto, January, 1973